Recovering My Lost Pieces

Ulyssa Cook

Recovering My Lost Pieces
Copyright 2023 by Uylssa Cook

Publisher: Smarti Publishing & Co., LLC

All rights reserved. No part of this publication may be reproduced, distributed, or transmitted in any form or by any means, including photocopying, recording, or other electronic or mechanical methods without the prior written permission of the publisher, except in the case of brief quotations embodied in critical reviews and certain other noncommercial uses permitted by copyright law.

For permission requests, write to the publisher addressed. "Attention: Permissions Coordinator," at the address below.

authorucook@gmail.com
smartipublishing21@gmail.com

ISBN: 979-8-9865690-3-1 (Paperback)

Cover Art: By Smarti Designs, LLC

Acknowledgments

I want to, first, dedicate this book to My Lord Yeshua for all he has done for me.
Thank you To My husband, Joseph Cook, and kids Latoya, Sharmika, Zenobia, and Sarah.

My best and dear friends Jessica Jones and Jacquline Moore. My photographer Wali Cooper and my Publisher, Tia Knight, with Smarti Publishing and Co. Thank you all for your help.

I would also like to thank my mentors in ministry and encouragers: Dr. Allen and Bishop Dunn.

Last but certainly not least, the memory of my beautiful parents, James and Linda Turner.

Index

Copyright

Acknowledgments

Chapter 1............................... Dealing with Dysfunction

Chapter 2............... My First Encounter with Being Different

Chapter 3............................ The Seed Planted

Chapter 4............................. Uncovering My Past

Chapter 5............................ New Place and The Old Me

Chapter 6..................... The Consequences of an Open Door

Chapter 7.............................. Recovering My Lost Pieces

Dealing With Dysfunction!

I was blessed to be born in New York in 1967 on a cold winter day. However, I never knew my life would turn out as it did. Being a young lady in the great city was incredible. I was blessed with two great parents. My dad was an excellent provider for us. He worked hard and was always a supportive father. He was such a quiet, sweet gentleman; we knew he meant business whenever he yelled, so we listened without hesitation. It was funny how he had one personality, and my mom had the opposite.

We never knew what to expect from her. She would be happy one minute and mad the next. Dad did all he could to keep the peace, but it did not work, especially when Mom did not get her way. I learned early in life that if you want something, get mad and manipulate until you get your way. Some people never want to admit it, but half of our learning comes from our upbringing. I will never forget how my mom wanted a bigger vehicle. So, she convinced us to tell Daddy we did not have much room to move in the station wagon. Within a few months, my dad got us a van.

Looking back on it now, I see how we saw things but did not understand and ended up following what we were taught. I wonder if people understand what they are doing to their kids when they teach them wrong things. For example, my mom would say it's wrong to lie; But when someone would call for her, and she did not want to deal with them, she would tell us to say she was not home. How can you tell me not to lie but show me it is okay for you to do it? This little example does not seem significant, but it can be big.

Another example is that we were told to be honest but saw our parents as dishonest. These little things always stay in my mind. I thought, why are you doing it if you tell me not to do it? Shouldn't the rules be the same for you? Some people may see things differently, but I always wanted to know why people do or don't do what they say but expect the opposite from you. So seriously, consider this; we will recognize some mistakes we make as parents.

My life in New York was simple but fun. I can remember the first business my dad started that my mom ran most of the time while he worked. He instilled such good values in us. We were able to work in the store, and when payday came, we all got a little piece of the pie. We combined a bait store and a furniture store; the second floor was where we lived. It was actually a nice place with three bedrooms, a kitchen, and a bathroom. My dad instilled in us to pay our bills first, save a little and then play with the rest. These simple instructions are a blessing until this very day.

Like most kids, we all had chores, and my mom expected them to be completed right after you did your homework, and then you could play. I will never forget the YMCA was having a community day, and I wanted to go so badly. I asked mommy, and she was fine with it if I did my homework, then my chores, and I was free to go. My mom was leaving, so I told her I got it covered. Right before she left, she told me to make sure that once I finished cleaning up to come downstairs and do a few other things, like dump the dirty water in the backyard before I left. She specifically instructed me not to toss the water out of the window on the second floor. Now I heard her, but I really did not hear her. I thought everything would be about to be over at the YMCA by the time I finished my chores. So, I then came up with what I considered a good plan to get this done in five minutes so I could go and play.

I figured it would be much quicker if I cleaned downstairs and then went upstairs. So, I got to work, and the first floor was cleaned in three minutes. I figured let's do a spot here and there, and if needed, I will come back on another day to finish it up. It's funny because as I think about it, she knew I was not gonna do it the way she told me. It was a setup, and I fell for it. Once I got upstairs, I began to clean. The list she gave was long; I could not skip it because I knew she would notice. Man! It took twenty minutes! All I could think of was the fun I was missing. So finally, I finished. I thought, *I am gonna just throw this water out the window, and I am done*! So, I pushed up the window and tossed this greasy water out of the window. I heard a loud yell, "who threw that water on me?" I realized someone was walking by, and the hot greasy water fell on somebody's head. I closed the window, ran downstairs, and went out the back door. I figured it would be alright if the person did not know that it was me. Since no one was home but me, who was gonna say anything?

So I went to the YMCA, and oh, it was a blast; I had so much fun. When I got home, my mom was waiting for me at the front door. She looked fine, so I figured all was well. She opened the door and waited to go upstairs. I did not even realize I was walking into a heated event. I was the one getting ready to be baked. My mom waited until I got my PJs on and asked me what had happened. I looked at her like I had no idea what she was talking about and responded, "Ma'am?"

She looked at me and said, "I TOLD YOU NOT TO TOSS THAT WATER OUT THE WINDOW, DIDN'T I?"

I looked at her and said, "Yes, that is what you said."

She then asked, "Why was there a girl waiting for me when I got here? She told me someone threw some hot greasy water on her from the second floor." My face just dropped, and my eyes got big. I figured I was about to get a terrible whipping. Mommy looked at me and said, "That girl will be back tomorrow," She told me, "You will explain to her tomorrow morning why you did what you did to her." That was a long night. I could not sleep. I just kept thinking; *this girl is going to beat me up.*

Morning came, and I was a nervous wreck. Finally, around 8:30 am, I heard the girl tell me to come downstairs. My mom said, "You better beat her good, or you will have to deal with me."

I thought, "I do not want to fight; maybe she and I can just talk."

So, I walked downstairs, and there was a huge girl. She looked six feet tall to me, and she was fluffy.

I thought, "This is not going to be good."

I tried apologizing to the girl, but she just put her fist up and said, "Come on."

I was trying so hard to avoid this, but my mom came to the door, and She and the girl started calling each other names.

I thought, *now, this is too much*! I just wanted to keep the peace.

That girl called my mom terrible names, and my mom returned the fire! Then my mom told the girl I was gonna beat her up. Shaking like a leaf, I soon realized that talking was not gonna fix this one. So, I fought the girl, and the more she called me names, the more upset I was! Of course, my mom was not helping at all. I can't say I won because who really wins when you fight? I felt so bad because I realized that this could have been avoided if I had just listened. I learned such a lesson that day, remembering that every action has a reaction.

A week later, Mommy was working, and we were home alone. This was never a good idea. We stayed into things all the time. My siblings and I decided we wanted to bowl, so we got my mom's bowling ball out of the corner and began to bowl. My little brother had a bright idea.

He said, "We really need something for the bowling pens." We looked around and thought, *what can we get*? In the corner were my mom's favorite perfume bottles. These were classic, shaped like cars, and she had ten. We never thought that it would not be good if that bowling ball hit that glass. So, we lined them up and began to bowl. The first hit knocked a wheel off one of the bottles, and a little perfume leaked. I thought this might not be a good idea, but we figured we would be okay if we did not hit them hard.

It was my time, and I wanted a strike, so I rolled the ball and smashed three of my mom's perfume cars. Right after, we heard our parents pulling up. I took the three bottles I busted and hid them. When my parents came home, we didn't realize a sweet aroma was in the house. Mommy opened the door, and all we heard was cursing. "WHAT ARE Y'ALL DOING?"

"Nothing!"

"Have you been in my perfume?"

Being smart, I yelled, "We wasted it by accident."

We were okay for a day or two, but when she found the three broken bottles, we realized life might be over for us. So, my mom lined us up and began beating us. Of course, I got it worse because I was the oldest; I didn't know better, and most of it was my ideal. Boy, I tell you, it is funny now, but back then, we were terrified. It is amazing as I look back.

Family rides were the best. I remember us going to Canada and just having fun. We went to the park, and as we were playing, I found a dead momma rat with some babies near her. I was not thinking, so don't judge me for this. Hey, I was just a kid! I thought, "these babies gonna die if they stay here." I figured I would raise them and then set them free. I got a box and put the four little rats in it to carry them home and take care of them. Once we were riding, I kept the box close to me so no one would know what I was doing. Because it was a long trip, when we got home, I was asleep. I figured I would just get them in the morning and bring them into the house. Well, when I got up in the morning, Daddy had taken the car and left with it to go to work. That evening when he got home, I had forgotten all about the box with the rats in it. Well, a week passed, and we were riding to the store; my dad said,

"What's that smell in this car?"

I did not even add up that the rats were dead and now stinking. We got back home, and Daddy left to go wash the car. When he got back, he sat us down and asked if any of us had something to tell him. We all looked at each other and were like, no. Daddy told us he found three dead rats in a box and wanted to know which one of us did it. I told him that the rats I put in the box were alive, so they could not be the same rats. Daddy then asked me how long it had been. I smiled and said,

"A week ago."

I told him how I found them at the park. The momma was dead, so I was gonna raise them and then set them loose. Daddy then told me the dead rats were the ones I left in the car. He explained that they could not survive if I did not feed them and if the vehicle was hot every day. I just cried and said,

"No, I was gonna save their lives!"

Yeah, I admit it does not make sense now, but I had a plan back then. I realize my plans keep getting me into a lot of trouble.

If you think about it, some of those good ideas you had got you into a lot of trouble. I always tried to do things to help, but it just did not work out this way for me.

Learning That I Am Different

Our house in New York was very different from others. The huge three-story house was strange, and I always saw things. For a long time, I thought something was wrong with me. No one saw the things I did, and I really thought maybe it was me that had issues. We were so blessed to have our own rooms in this house. My brother lived in the basement, my sister and I had the second floor, and our parents were on the third floor. One day my brothers were getting ready to go to their room from the second-floor door. When my brothers opened the door, I saw fire shooting out of the opening. I just stared at it to make sure I was really seeing fire. I told my brothers not to go down the stairs because there was a fire. They just looked back at me and laughed as they said you are crazy.

I screamed, "Don't go down there! It's on fire."

My brothers just turned, looked at me, and then went down the stairs. That was a long night for me. I could not sleep thinking about my brothers. I even told my parents, and they went to check on them. Daddy said they were good and told me to go back to bed. The next morning, I was so glad to see them; I gave both of them a big hug, and I figured, well, I guess I was just seeing things, but it was so real. I tried not to think about it, but I was on the third floor a few days later and saw a massive figure in the attic. It was something I could not describe. The crazy thing is no one saw it but me, so I just figured something was wrong with my eyes again. This was the beginning of many strange things happening in my life, and it had me to the point when I saw something I did not tell anyone.

On weekends, I spent a lot of time with my grandma. She would come and pick me up for church. It was fun, but even there, I would see things and start thinking, *what is wrong with me?*

I never thought about why I was the only child that went with Grandma. I just figured my other siblings were not interested in going to church. But I will never forget one day, the speaker was talking, and I had to look at him twice. He had one face, but one side was black, and the other was white, and every time he spoke, spider webs came out of his mouth. Things really started getting crazy from there. I tried to tell my grandma, but she just told me she would take me to check my eyes. Sleeping at night was not good for me. I would see things all night long. I stopped telling people because I was only seen as a child with a big imagination. It is amazing how the devil was slowly shutting down my gift. If I question it, then there is no way I would be comfortable telling others. So, time went on, and I did not say much about what I saw because I did not understand it, and no one was around to help me with what was happening. I discovered the truth years later, but we will get to that in a few more chapters.

One day I went fishing with my grandma and her friend Johnny. Lock Ten was a huge lake where the big navy ships came, and the area where we would fish was high up on a hill. I was fishing, and I was far from the dock. I was minding my business with my pole in the water, and I felt something push me. I looked around and saw nothing, so I just kept fishing. My grandma told me not to get close to the dock, and I told her I would not. Then suddenly again, I felt another push and another; before I knew it, I fell over the dock. I don't remember much, but my grandma told me they ran down the hill worrying about finding me in such a big mass of water. Grandma told me she knew only God did this for me. She said when they got to the area close to where they could see the water. She noticed that my sandals were caught on a tree in the water; this kept me from going under. I cannot tell you how long I was in that water or even how I felt or what I was thinking. I remember being pulled out and my grandma fussing at me.

"Didn't I tell you not to get close to the dock?"

"It was not me, but something that kept pushing me." She just looked at me and said,

"You need to stop with those lies and listen to people!"

I did not realize until recently, forty years later, that this incident had me scared of bridges and a severe fear of crossing them. I feared falling into the water. Now I know someone reading this may not understand what was going on. I did not see what was pushing me. I knew that something was doing it. I did not get it then, but now I see. The enemy wanted me dead because of the gift in me from the beginning. So, he tried to kill me. You see, my life was designed to be a blessing to many, but the enemy needed to put blocks in my life so I would never recover the pieces he took from me at an early age. I had one experience after another.

For instance, one day in New York, I was walking to the store by Grandma Queen's house to get some candy from the store. It was a nice day, the sun was out, and you could see the road well. I am at the corner about to cross the street. I waited for the walking signal, and as soon as I looked, I did not see a car coming, but when I got into the middle of the road, a taxi came out of nowhere. It hit me so hard that I remember falling across the street and hitting the ground. When I came to, I was in the hospital again, and my head was wrapped up. I could not speak or move. I heard my parents talking about a drunk driver that ran the stop light and hit me. This took a while for me to get over. My jaw, my leg, and several of my teeth were broken. For months I could only eat baby food and soft things. I received physical and speech therapy to learn to walk and talk again. Once I got myself together, I thought I needed to be in a bubble to stay safe. Luckily for me, all these situations of getting hurt calmed down a little. Until we decided to go sliding on the street one day after an ice storm.

    New York was famous for nice ice storms and snowstorms. We could dig tunnels through all the snow we got. It was like a holiday for us! We had so many snow days that school did not get closed. It was normal for us! People just put chains on their tires, and we keep things moving. Usually, when it snowed, we would get boxes and slide on the snow. There was a hill by our house, and my siblings and I thought it would be nice to slide down it in the snow like we were in an actual ice race. The problem was that the hill was fenced in, and it had a huge wall around it. My siblings and I thought this would be fun.

    Oh, don't judge us! We were kids that stayed busy, and we were always into stuff. So, we get to the hill, and as we are going to the top. I had a great plan. Yeah, you heard me; I had a great plan! I told my siblings that we would not hit the wall. If we got close enough to each other, it would lessen the blow. Oh, it was fun, and my plan worked well. Until…My little brother wanted to look out and see how close we were to the wall. The next thing we knew, he had hit the wall and split his head open. It wasn't a lot, but just a little, enough for us to be back in the ER. It was getting so bad that the staff in the ER learned our names. My little brother ended up with 12 stitches. It was a good battle scar; we treated him like a king so he would not tell what happened. It's easy to write this now that both of our parents are gone, but honey, if Linda Ann was here, I would get a beat down just for the things we did that she did not know about. My siblings and I truly enjoyed our youth. The fun and the memories are too many to tell but trust me, it was a lot, and we always had fun.

The Seed Planted

There are times when we really do not understand why things happen to us. It's easy to see now that I was set up early to fail, but God. In New York, there were good times as well as bad times. Let me explain. The only time anybody watched us, other than our mom, was when she went to work. We were the kind of kids you just could not leave alone. I will never forget a relative who would watch us when my mom was at work. We played games with him, and we really enjoyed it when he came to watch us until he changed on me one day. He told us he wanted to play a new game called "Go and Get." We were like, okay, how do we play this game? It sounded fun. He explained that each person would hide, and whoever found them would get whatever that person asked for.

So, the game began, and we all hid. When he found me, he told me he only wanted a kiss from his favorite cousin. I laughed, and it was different when I went to kiss him. He pulled me close to him and held me, and I felt really uncomfortable. It is hard to explain, but I felt this was not a friendly kiss. After dealing with this situation, I decided to set out for the next game. The next week he came back to watch us again, and he wanted to play this game again. I was hesitant because it seemed that I was the only person he found when we played this game. This time we went and hid again, and when he found me, he requested to put his hand in my pants. I really wondered why he wanted to do that. I could not see how that was fun. I asked him why he wanted to do that, and he said I agreed to play, and I had to let him do what he wanted. So, I let him put his hands in my pants. He seemed to really like it, but I was like, okay, it felt good, but I just do not get it. The week after, we had a family gathering, and he was there. Now I really was uncomfortable being around him. One day I went to a family function, and he was always around me. It seemed like he was staring at me every time I moved. I figured it was best to go into the house, and when I went to sit down there, he came. He really had me freaking out because the stare he gave me was just creepy. I noticed he was gone, so I went to the bathroom. As soon as I opened the door, he came out of the bathroom. I just looked at him and went in to do my business. A few minutes later, I noticed he opened the door and said,

"Excuse me, I left something in here,"

I said, "You can get it when I am finished!"

Then he locked the door and started licking me in my private area. I had never felt anything like it. After that day, this became a weekly occurrence, and I began to like it. One day he told me he wanted to try something different, and that was the first time he penetrated me. Until that day, he had only played with me by doing oral sex and putting his fingers in my private area. Here I am, a nine-year-old child, thinking, why is he doing this? Then he told me it had to be our secret because he did not want me to get into trouble for doing this. I really thought I would get in trouble.

I remember he said, "You agreed to play, so I can do what I want."

I felt like I had allowed this by agreeing to a game that went too far. As a child that has dealt with this, I can see how kids feel responsible. A predator will have his prey thinking they participated willingly, making them partly responsible for what was happening.

It may not make sense to everyone, but you have to remember I was a child, and what a child cannot do is rationalize things like an adult. The seed was planted, and I was obsessed with oral sex from that day forward. I started looking forward to seeing him; I would do whatever he wanted as long as he did that. One day my parents went out of town for the weekend, and we were all staying in separate places; he was my babysitter. That weekend I went to a dark place I had never been to before. It got so bad that sex was now an obsession, and I wanted it all the time. I understand now that when a door is open at the wrong time, it can cause many issues in your life, which is what happened to me. I was now a young freak and was getting worse by the day. These issues became some of my biggest challenges. See, it only takes one problem in your life to change everything. I dealt with this for years, and it had total control over me.

    The time came when my father made us aware that we would move to Virginia to help care for my grandfather. I thought this was the time for me to try and start over. This seemed to be a good idea, but the only issue was that *I was going with me when I moved*. People judge folks with issues. I wonder if they have ever questioned what the root is of the issue the person has. People are not designed to be bad; the things that happen to them make them bad. So here I am, at nine years old, scared of bridges and obsessed with sex due to traumatic experiences, and the issues of my life were about to get worse.

    I now see that this was when pieces of my life went missing. This came to me when I sat down to put a puzzle together, and when I thought I was almost finished, I could not find a few of the pieces. I had a revelation at that moment. I then realized this puzzle was how my life was, and I had to start looking to see where the lost pieces were. It took me years to connect what really was going on. But now I am seeing as I put the missing pieces in the puzzle of my life, the picture of who I really am is starting to form clearly.

Uncovering The Past

Most of my life I spent with my grandmother as a child. She always had a lesson to teach me. I listened, but sometimes I thought her advice was strange. To me, she was such a wonderful woman. When we moved to Virginia, I truly missed her. I tried to keep in touch with her as much as possible, but being a teenager made that hard. I noticed that my mom really did not like her mom. I would ask her about going to see Grandma, and she would get so mad at me. It was strange, but things make sense as I now learn about my history. My mom, as she aged, became a sweeter person. I actually enjoyed being around her. Don't get me wrong, we had years of issues. I was closer to my dad than my mom.

As my parents got older, my dad was placed in a nursing home due to problems with his feet, and needed rehabilitation. My mom treated him poorly as he got older and got sicker. I enjoyed the times I would go and see him at the nursing home. He told me so many stories and would make a joke that was not funny but just laughed so hard. Even though the joke was not funny, his laugh made you want to join him because he got so tickled. I did not appreciate that at the time, but now that he is gone, I value those days. We laughed a lot as he told me more about the family history. One day I asked him how he and my mom met, and he just laughed at me. Daddy asked me,

"Did you realize I am 17 years older than your mom?"

I told him, "Yes." but I just figured they fell in love at an early age. My dad made me aware that he was dating my grandmother. At first, I just looked at him and shook my head, *like what!* He repeated it,

"I should have been your grandfather." I looked at him and asked,

"So, what happened?"

He told me that he and Mommy started messing around, and then she became pregnant. He did the honorable thing, and they got married. I asked him how Grandma felt about that, and he said,

"Oh, we were not that serious, so she was fine."

He then told me that Mommy was very promiscuous, and she got around. I asked him how they ended up living in New York, and what he said to me next blew me away. Daddy made me aware that Grandma had gotten pregnant by the milkman, and her husband was furious, so she moved to New York with her sister to live. I asked him if the milkman was black, and he said no. That explained a lot about my aunt. She was very, very light-skinned. I always wondered why, but I never asked anyone. If you knew my mom, that would surely have been a beatdown. So, I started figuring this out and am putting part of this puzzle together. I just found out my grandmom and mom were both promiscuous, and my Aunt Jean was killed in New York by her pimp. I was putting my family issues in front of me and understanding why I was dealing with so much. Some do not realize that generational curses are real. I wanted to learn about my past to see if my life was a repeated cycle of my family history.

A few days before my dad passed away, I went to see him, and he was not talking, just resting in bed. A few days before, he told me he had seen his funeral, which bothered him. I told my dad that dying is not bad if you have Christ in your life. He told me,

"Sometimes people do so much that even Christ cannot forgive them."

I then told him," That is not true. He can and will forgive anyone if they are genuine and sincere when they repent."

On his death, I took my mom to see him, and the doctor was there. I asked him how he was doing, and he told me,

"We are keeping him comfortable."

Many folks may say that sounds good, but being a nurse, I knew what that meant. So, Mommy and I went to see him, and he was not talking. He was lying on his right side, not speaking. I then called my siblings and told them I needed everyone to get to the nursing home. That was December 31st; as all the family gathered around, he started looking at us. It was when my granddaughter Keekee came into the room. He looked up and started carrying on a conversation. My sister and I just looked at each other and smiled. I asked him if he was thirsty, and he said yes, so we went and got his favorite chocolate milkshake. That was the last time he ate anything. My sister told him she would check into her room and then return. He nodded his head, and she left. I really felt that he did not want her to see him pass. My dad would never do anything to upset my sister. She was gone for about ten minutes, and I noticed his breathing was changing. Then he looked up and closed his eyes peacefully with a great big smile on his face. I can still see it right now! The man that was like Superman to me was gone.

After the funeral, I realized that my mom could not take care of herself, so I started to check on her more. I would make doctor appointments for her, and she would call and cancel them. I laugh at it now because she knew she was sick, but she did not want us kids to find out. Now one thing I can tell you about my mom is that she was a force of her own, and no one was going to tell Linda what to do. So, my younger brother moved in with her. For a while, that went well, but they kept butting heads. I will never forget one day she and I were out riding and chatting. I had asked her about going to see Grandma for her 91st birthday. She got fussy and then asked me why I wanted to go and see that woman, but she did not say it that nicely. I asked her what the issue was and why she did not like her momma. She told me,

"That woman put me through a lot of stuff."

I looked at her and said, "Mom, that woman, your momma?"

and she stated, "That's all she did was birth me."

I said, "Mom, how can you say that?"

Then the truth came out. My mom had held it in for over 69 years that she hated her mom because she made her have an abortion when she got pregnant at 14 years old. I said,

"Mom, you were young, and she was trying to take care of you. She probably felt she could not take care of another child."

Mom looked at me, and she began to cry.

"That does not matter; she should have at least considered me."

She then told me something that just shocked me. Mommy looked at me and said, "She doesn't love you; she just feels guilty."

I asked her, "What was she talking about?" and she told me she carried her to also get an abortion when she was pregnant. My eyes got big, and I was like, "What do you mean?" She told me that grandma took her at 15 years old to get an abortion while pregnant with me. She said she would never forget that lady pushing that clothes rack up her, and she thought she got rid of me like she had gotten rid of my sister a year ago. I just held my stomach and sat down. Mommy looked at me and said,

"Now you see why I can't stand her."

I had to get myself together, and then I told her,

"We all have made mistakes we wish we did not do; we must learn to forgive and forget."

She looked at me and said, "I will never forgive her for that."

So now the puzzle of my life is getting more pieces on it. For years I never felt incomplete and that no one loved me. You may not understand this, but when that clothes rack was placed into my mom, it gave me a spirit of rejection. Even though Mommy was not trying to get rid of me, the act was significant enough to affect me. Ladies, everything you do when you are pregnant affects the baby in your womb. Kids now walk around feeling rejected because their moms did not know. When they found out the baby was a girl and they wanted a boy, that disappointment was transferred to that fetus. That baby is not even here, but it can be affected by the mom's emotions because that baby is attached to her.

My mom said one thing that really got my attention. She told me that she took Daddy from Grandma, and it was her way to pay her back for the pain she caused her.

I said, "WOW!" "You tried to hurt her but missed having a relationship with your mom."

She then told me that as Daddy got older, she was upset with him because he would not leave his family. I tell you, when you try to get back at people, it only hurts you. When we do not learn to forgive and try to take matters into our own hands, we can make a bigger mess than we had initially. My mom carried this for years, and now I understand all her bitterness. She allowed a sore to form into an infection that affected her entire body.

I asked her, "When was the last time you were happy?"

She paused, looked at me, and said, "My happiness stopped at 9 years old when my cousin molested me."

I sat there thinking about my mom and her history of drinking. She was a bitter and nasty woman all because of her past.

People would judge her, and even we kids could not see why she was the way she was. But really, she was a wounded woman who never healed. When a person has a wound that does not heal, that will affect the entire body. My mom had placed herself on a trauma trip, and it was killing her. I tried my best to get her to spend more time with her grandkids and get out. I will never forget when I carried her to a gospel concert with Shirley Caesar and Lee Williams. This was the first time I saw her really enjoy herself. She laughed and sang as some of her favorite songs were performed by the artist she liked. After the concert, we went out to eat. It gave me such joy to see her enjoying life that day. I watched and saw her become a sweet, loving woman. She even apologized one day when she stayed with me and cursed at my husband. I was shocked that I had seen her apologize, and she cried and told me it was so peaceful in my house. I was like, "Mom, what do you mean?"

She smiled and said, "You'll don't fuss; it's quiet and calm here."

I told her, "I like peace and quiet."

She laughed and said, "I only thought this kind of stuff happened on tv."

It became my goal to spend more time with her and tell her about the love of Christ. This woman that I thought was so mean I now saw her in a different light. Life was rough for her. She was alive, but she was not living. I am trying to say that there is such a thing as being alive but just going through the motions. It's a task to get up every day. God wants us to enjoy the time he gave us here and not be stuck because of the issues that may have us trapped in quicksand. Yes, I said it, trapped! The more you move, the more you sink.

New Place And The Old Me

Living in the country was fun. We had good times just living a simple life. After my grandfather passed, years went by, and my issues started to bloom again. At the age of fifteen, I was pregnant; now that I think of it, my mom was fifteen and pregnant with me. I did not know what I was getting into when the young man asked me to marry him. So now here I am, young with a baby and a husband. Thank God for my mom and mother In love; they helped me as I went to school and took care of my baby girl. Things were going well. My hubby was working, and I was about to graduate, so we moved out independently. This is when things hit the fan.

When you live with someone, you never realize the struggle until you get your own place. So here we are now on our second child. I am working, but my hubby was hanging out a lot. I was not too upset, but it got so he never had money to pay bills. I then noticed that our bank account stayed in the negative. I eventually realized he was taking checks from the middle of the checkbook. I was not aware that he was addicted to drugs at the time. I really thought he was cheating on me. He seemed emotionally abusive when he could not get out and get his "stuff." Years went by, and we lost a lot of things. I will never forget we were about to get our income tax check, and I was so glad the furniture bill was due. I figured we could pay the bill off. My husband got to the check, and the next thing I knew, he put the money down on a red car. So, we lost our furniture, and there was no food in the house. I finally got to the point where I was just fed up and ready to leave.

One night my husband got drunk, and he came home. I had fixed his favorite meal, pig feet, potato salad, and greens. He was so drunk he took the plate and threw the hot plate on me, and I was amazed! That night we were in bed, and in the middle of the night, I felt a cold spot in the bed. I got up and realized the bed was wet on his side and had spread to my side. I woke him up, and he just looked at me and said, "I did it."

He then got up and made me lie in the wet spot, and he went and changed his clothes. Here, I have more missing pieces in my life. Just look at this: I experienced abuse, finding out I was supposed to be aborted, the fear of bridges, being rejected as an infant, sexual issues, and emotional abuse. Now, as I look at this, I see how the devil strategically broke me down by overwhelming me with issues. If you really do an inventory of your life, you will see a similar pattern. The next day I left and went to my Godmother's house. She stayed by the church that I attended. I was just fed up. My husband also knew I spent a lot of time in church.

One day I was getting ready for service, and my pastor called me to make me aware that my husband was at the church with the police looking for us. He had reported that we were missing. My pastor asked me if I would come and talk with him. I agreed to go to the church to meet him so the police would know I was not missing. I drove to the church by myself. I did not bring the kids with me. Pastor, he, and I went into the office to talk. The pastor told my husband he would have to learn not to throw things at me and that he would one day be a deacon in the church. My husband laughed and said, "That will be the day I lose my mind." I did not go home that day. I really wanted to see if he was really ready to change.

I started attending church more during this time, which helped some but also hindered me. The crazy thing is we were told we needed to be saved, but no one really explained what that was. So, one day, I got saved! I was told I was a new creature in Christ, and the old things had passed away. I figured this was good. God has taken all my issues away, and now I can be a better person. No one explains that you will have to release those past issues. Remember, God does not force us to do anything. I did well for a while until I met people in church that were just as broken as myself. You are drawn to these people when you have similar issues. Hubby and I began to try and work things out. So, he started coming to church, and we would talk after service. We did get back together but with more rules about what I wanted from him. For a while, things went well, and then it started all over again. He was not as bad, but I noticed he was spending money on things and not helping with the house bills this time. Things did get better, but it took time, and I dealt with my personal issues during this time.

I stepped out of my marriage, and this was not my intention. When one has not dealt with personal issues and their home life is not good, they should be careful about who they talk to about what they are going through. Here I am at work, and one of my co-workers starts to tell me how his marriage is going. I tell him how my marriage is going. We then begin assisting one another with each other's issues. This was the biggest mistake of my life. *How can two bleeding people stop a hemorrhage?* It got so that I could rely on this guy to give me money when I needed it. We would bring snacks to each other and go out to lunch. Not realizing we were starting a fire that would need to be dealt with eventually.

One day my car broke down, and I asked my husband to help me get to work. He told me he was too busy and that I needed to call in. I did not want to call in and say I was sick when I was not sick. So, I called the guy to tell him I needed a ride; he met me and took me to work. He became the backup person I could always count on, and I realized that was not good. The day I broke my marriage vow, my husband and I had a heated discussion. He had taken the light bill money and bought something, and the lights got turned off. I was so upset I went to meet this guy crying. He hugged me, told me it was okay, and that he would help me whenever he could. Before I knew it, that hug turned into a kiss, and he started groping me. The next thing I knew, he was doing that thing I liked. Yes, you got it, *that thing*. That was the day I walked away from my marriage. I realized that I needed to stop what I was doing, but this person had become more of a crutch. I could always rely on him.

    I don't know if you have ever experienced wanting to stop doing something but being too scared to actually do it; that is how it was for me. I kept thinking about how I would make it without this man's help. I was not proud of what I did. When a person is wounded, they cannot act like they don't have a problem. This bothered me because I could not figure out how God would let me get into something like this. I was wearing a long skirt and a long shirt on the outside, and I looked like I was saved, but in actuality, I was only fixing the outside; I did not let God come in and fix the inside of me. I really felt like I was a big disappointment to God. I must have done something wrong for him to leave me. I thought long and hard about this. We now have churches full of people with unresolved issues trying to make it. The problem is that people are trying to solve their problems without God.

    I dealt with this for years and began to change once I found a church that started peeling off the years and layers of hurt, pain, and neglect I had suffered. People will label folks who do not seem to be getting it, but I realize now that many churches are just going through a format. People have issues and need the word and teaching to help them. The church is supposed to be a spiritual hospital; many people come in with alcohol or drug issues and can't get the help they need. The church will treat that person like they are contagious and avoid them. It is time for the Body of Christ to care for the other parts of the body. I would watch the preacher preach, and at the end of the service, they would give me their phone number to hook up with them. If you go to church, I encourage you to realize that there is no perfect person; we are all in a hospital looking for Jesus to heal and fix us. It's when you get a substitute for an issue and cause more problems. So, instead of having one problem, I had two, and I could not blame anyone because I caused this myself. Just because it was not intentional, that does not make it right.

  As time passed, I decided I would stop cheating physically, but we could have phone sex. At least then, I thought, I was not sinning and could still get that satisfaction. It's amazing how we rationalize doing wrong so we don't feel bad. It took time, but I realized that partial sin is still sin. So, where do I go from here? I could not stop myself, so what's next? Healing did not come until I had a genuine conversation with God and became honest with him. I asked God to come into my broken, scared heart. I cried out to him and asked him if he would help me, and I told him that I would also try to help others. It took time, and I did slip, but I did repent and would tell God how I messed up because I did not seek his guidance. Oh, the devil tried to torment me. He told me how bad I was, how much of a failure I was, and I sometimes agreed with him. But I also told him the person that made me could fix me.

  So, I accepted my issues and placed myself in God's hands. When old feelings came up, I would remind myself of all the tears, pain, and hurt I went through the last time I allowed my flesh to take over. I continually thought about how much I would hurt God if I cheated on him. Men would be calling me, dropping by my house and job. I would look at them and say, "This is a way to enjoy myself and have fun, but do I really want to deal with the consequences that will come after a few minutes of fun." I learned that hell was forever, and a few minutes could make or cancel a reservation there. Eventually, I saw the consequences were not worth it, and I continued to move forward.

The Consequence Of An Open The Doors

Now that I have given my life to Christ, I see things better. Most people may not understand this, but I always wanted to know why I did what I did and where it came from. As I review my history, I am putting things together, and I see this is not a coincidence. A lot of the issues that I went through, my mom went through. History repeats itself, and if someone does not change history, it will be passed down to the next generation. I want to inform my sisters that many of our issues are combinations of our past. If you look deep into your history, you will see that your bloodline (unintentionally) passed down a lot of stuff. Today my mom, my dad, and my grandma are all gone. My grandmother never knew that my mom had passed away. If people thought about what they did before they did it and how it will affect the future, some people might think before they act.

There is a story in the bible about King David. He got a woman pregnant, and she was a man's wife in his army. King David called the man back home so he would sleep with his wife to cover his tracks so no one would know what he had done. He thought he had gotten away with it until God sent a prophet named Nathan to reveal what King David had done was wrong. The baby he made with this woman would die. He also stated that he would have issues with his family because of his sin. One problem caused many different problems in his family line. David had a son named Amnon that raped his sister Tamar. His son Absalom killed his brother Amnon after he raped their sister. Then he had a son named Solomon, that had multiple wives, and they caused him to turn away from God. His son Absalom tried to take the Kingdom from him. King Saul tried numerous times to kill David. Some doors we open can take us a lifetime to close.

What my life has taught me is that the process takes time. I did not get into this overnight, and it may take some time to recover. I am also more patient with ladies that are dealing with issues. You must understand their pain to really get why they are where they are. Now that God has put me into ministry, my passion is to help women who have been hurt and left by themselves to try and figure out how they will deal with life. Even Jesus forgave the woman caught in adultery. *Have you ever wondered where the man was?* If she was caught in the act, a man was somewhere in the picture. Our society looks at women as if they do these sexual acts alone. If a man sleeps around, the guys congratulate him, but the woman is considered a whore.

Does this make sense? Why is one party less guilty than the other if it takes two? There was a custom in my past church where if a young girl got pregnant, they would bring her before the church to confess her sins. I have always had an issue because she did not get pregnant alone. When Jesus saw this woman had messed up, he stooped down on the ground and began writing. Jesus looked up with love and compassion and told the crowd that whoever was present who never messed up could throw the first stone. You see, if we are to be like Jesus, this should be our approach. Instead, *church folks* will throw stones after they have committed adultery and fornication in the past but soon forget where God has brought them from.

As you can see, this is a tender spot for me, I do not believe you should beat people down, but you should love them up. Many women I have talked to will not return to church because of how they are treated. Some people will have a lot to answer for because one thing Jesus did not do was push people away because of their issues. For anyone that is reading this and you went through this, I personally apologize. Please do not blame God for those in the church that need a reality check. God is a good God, and He does not condemn. All He wants is for you to repent and really seek him. You cannot fix yourself; only the manufacturer can repair you. And you need to go into the shop so he can work on you. Now I say this because as I am in ministry, I make sure no one in our church gets offended. We are not perfect, but if I ever get wind that someone having an issue, I do not let it ride; I will go and talk with that person. There is nothing worse than coming to the spiritual hospital, and you leave worse than when you were when you came in.

Please get up and go back to God. He will forgive you, and he will show you love. He did it for me! Honey, I was a woman mistreated by my mistakes by *church folks.* God is in no way in this picture, and no one can tell me differently. Just remember that every action will have a reaction. Always look first at what you are about to do, how it may affect your reputation, and how people will see you. Then think about how it will affect your kids, if you have any, or how it will affect your family. Then think about how long it will take for you to fix this if it goes the wrong way. Way out the chances of what can happen, good and bad. And then, most importantly, how will this affect me spiritually, and what will it do to my relationship with God. Life is brief, and what you do here will determine where you will spend eternity. *Are five minutes of pleasure really worth it?* When you look at things this way, the way you do things will change. The nights I cried, men told me they loved me, and then they left; God was always there. He never left me, and he never pointed the finger at me. I have learned that God is truly faithful, and he will not leave me no matter what.

Consider what I am passing on to you. This is fifty-four years of learning, tears, and pain.

Recovering My Broken Pieces

I tried for years to figure out why I was the way I was, and now as I have begun recovering my pieces, things are more apparent. The process of putting my life back together started when I gave my heart to God. First, I needed to see that I was broken and I needed help. This took me over forty years to figure out. I pray and hope this will help someone so they will not have to go through what I went through. It's been hard, but I have learned some valuable lessons. Second, the next step of my life puzzle was to figure out where each piece of life would go. *Have you ever done a puzzle and placed a piece in the wrong spot?* You notice that you cannot complete the puzzle if it does not fit. Getting the whole story was what I needed to get my life puzzle started.

      Third, I needed to sort out the pieces where a corner piece could not go in the middle of the puzzle. I had to ensure that each piece went in the right place, or else the picture of my life would not be completed. I also needed to separate the pieces by color. Each color had to be in the place with the colors that would make the picture crystal clear to me. If you are doing a puzzle, you cannot put a piece of the eye in the slot where the mouth needs to be. Next, I needed to spread out the pieces to get a good view of what I was looking at. Sometimes just sitting back and looking at things helps you to visualize what the picture should look like and what parts go where. Lastly, as I began to concentrate and focus on life, I could see how the pieces looked, but they would not truly reveal my life image until I put them together. It took over fifty-four years to put my puzzle together. I know it seems like a long time, but do you know that some people are in their 60s and 70s and have not even begun to gather the pieces to see why their life is like it is.

I am sure as you read this that you have put a puzzle together or seen someone else put one together. Just imagine getting a puzzle with a lot of parts. Just think about it; this puzzle was gathered 54 years ago. There is no telling how many pieces I may have in all. Honestly, I cannot tell if I have all the pieces. Nothing is more frustrating than putting a puzzle together; in the end, you realize that a few pieces are missing. I'm trusting God that for any issues I cannot uncover, he will show me where the pieces are or make a piece to go in that vacant spot.

As I began this healing, I thank God, he did not allow me to become toxic as I was bleeding. Bleeding is a natural response when you have a wound; this is the healing process. The only thing to stop this healing phase is when you keep picking at the scab, and the wound cannot heal. This can cause inflammation, which is when bitterness sets in, and you cannot let the hurt and pain go. This makes me think about my mom. She really was a prisoner herself due to the issues of her past. If you do not treat the problem or look for help, it can cause you to be a person that will not love properly, isolate, and with whom no one can get along.

I pray that as you read this and if you have allowed inflammation to set in, this will be the beginning of your healing. Once you allow the process of healing to truly begin, you will then be able to see growth. It doesn't hurt when you think about what you have been through. You will be able to forgive and see that if a person causes this problem, they might have issues and need healing. The primary way to tell that you are in the final stages is when that thing comes up, or you see that person, it does not bother you anymore. I cannot begin to tell you the joy I now have as I began to start this puzzle. My scars and wounds are now healing; even though it is scary, I look forward to viewing my actual image.

For years I dealt with things so I wouldn't be rejected. I did things I did not like, fearing a person would reject me. I don't know if you have ever been there. That was my biggest fear! I tried to get everyone's approval because to be rejected again would have caused a setback for me. Only those that have been there would understand what I am saying. I needed man's approval so bad that I compromised. Now by doing this, I lost myself. I became an actor that played the part just so I could keep friends. Rejection from the wound was my trauma trap. I guess you wonder just what I am talking about.

People who have low self-esteem or fear of being rejected. Dread the thought of someone hating them or not wanting to be bothered with them. Sometimes I did things I never would do, but I compromised because I wanted so badly to fit in. Let me tell you, it bothered me; oh yes, I got gratification for a moment, but at what cost? I ended up being selfish and self-centered. So much so that I would do what I had to so people would stay in my circle. My turn around was when a girl tried to kiss me. Now I know people say this should not have been an issue, but there was one thing I detested, and that was it. I had to stand my ground; she talked bad about me and spread rumors. Then, as I prayed, I asked God why people couldn't get along and be friends. I then told him I was done. I was not dealing with people, which meant no more church for me. God allowed me to have my pity party for a while. Then one day, as I was listening to a song, I just broke down and lost it. I told God how he did not understand what I was going through. I have been rejected, mistreated, and taken advantage of. Again, he let me vent and have my pity party. Then in a soft still voice,

He whispered. "Why are you punishing me for what others do?"

I was like, "What? I'm not doing that!"

He said, "You're not talking to me. You stop singing and coming to church to spend time with me."

I told God it's not him; it's the people there. He then reminded me that everyone there was broken and that I could not expect broken glass not to cut me if I rubbed against it. I was just in awe. I asked God to forgive me and said I never meant to hurt him.

He told me he knew that, but I needed to realize that hurt people didn't know any better. I then realize that there is no such thing as church hurt. God does not hurt us; people do. So when issues arise in church or with people, just realize that if broken glass rubs against you, it makes you a victim too. I now know who has been there for me through all I have been through. Do not blame God for what people do. We have the right to make choices, and that sometimes impacts others. Never forget this, all my missing pieces came from my and others' mistakes. The best thing about this is that I can recover the pieces and fix or repair what is wrong or broken.

www.ingramcontent.com/pod-product-compliance
Lightning Source LLC
Chambersburg PA
CBHW070752050426
42449CB00010B/2438